Holy Places

Makkah

and other Islamic Holy Places

Mandy Ross

Heinemann
LIBRARY

08898984

H **www.heinemann.co.uk/library**
Visit our website to find out more information about **Heinemann Library** books.

To order:
☎ Phone 44 (0) 1865 888066
▤ Send a fax to 44 (0) 1865 314091
▭ Visit the Heinemann Bookshop at www.heinemann.co.uk/library to browse our catalogue and order online.

First published in Great Britain by Heinemann Library, Halley Court, Jordan Hill, Oxford OX2 8EJ, a division of Reed Educational and Professional Publishing Ltd. Heinemann is a registered trademark of Reed Educational and Professional Publishing Ltd.

OXFORD MELBOURNE AUCKLAND JOHANNESBURG BLANTYRE GABORONE IBADAN PORTSMOUTH NH (USA) CHICAGO

Designed by Joanna Sapwell and StoryBooks
Illustrations by Nick Hawken
Originated by Blenhiem Colour
Printed by Wing King Tong, Hong Kong, China

ISBN 0 431 15515 1
06 05 04 03 02
10 9 8 7 6 5 4 3 2 1

British Library Cataloguing in Publication Data
Ross, Mandy
     Makkah – (Holy places)
     1. Mecca – Saudi Arabia in Islam – Juvenile literature
     2. Islamic shrines – Juvenile literature 3. Mecca (Saudi Arabia)
     – Juvenile literature
     I.title
     297.3'52

Acknowledgements
The Publishers would like to thank the following for permission to reproduce photographs: Associated Press pp. 15, 27; Christine Osborne Pictures p. 9; Corbis p. 29; Popperfoto pp. 10, 14, 18, 19, 21; Robert Harding Picture Library p. 26; Trip/A Farago p. 28; Trip/H Rogers pp. 12, 23, 24, 25; Trip/Trip pp. 5, 6, 7, 8, 11, 13, 16, 17, 20.

Cover photograph reproduced with permission of The Stock Market.

Our thanks to Anita Ganeri for her assistance in the preparation of this book.

Every effort has been made to contact copyright holders of any material reproduced in this book. Any omissions will be rectified in subsequent printings if notice is given to the Publisher.

Contents

Words printed in bold letters, **like this**, are explained in the Glossary on page 30.

What is Makkah?

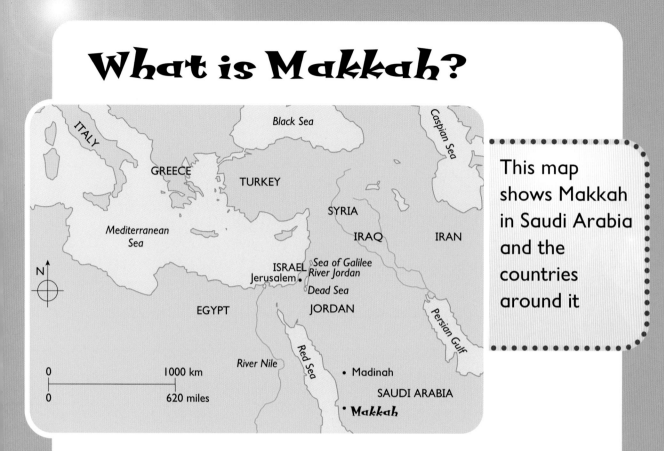

This map shows Makkah in Saudi Arabia and the countries around it

Makkah is the **holiest** city for Muslims, people who follow the **religion** of **Islam**. Makkah (also called Mecca) is in the country we now call Saudi Arabia, in the **Middle East**. All around the world, Muslims **pray** facing Makkah.

Makkah is important to Muslims because their **prophet** Muhammad (**pbuh**) was born there in 570 CE.

Every year, more than 2 million people make a holy journey or **pilgrimage** to Makkah. They say special prayers as they visit the holy places there. This pilgrimage is called **Hajj**. Every Muslim hopes to go on Hajj to Makkah at least once in his or her life.

What is Islam?

Islam is the religion followed by people called Muslims. Muslims pray to one God, **Allah**. They believe that Allah sent Muhammad (pbuh) to teach people how to live. The Muslim holy book is called the **Qur'an**.

The letters 'pbuh' stand for 'peace be upon him'. Muslims always say these words after Muhammad's name, to show their respect for him.

A Muslim place of worship is called a **mosque** (or sometimes masjid). Muslims always pray facing Makkah so each mosque is built to face the holy city.

Today Makkah is a modern city. It lies in a desert and is very hot and dry – it hardly ever rains there.

The modern city of Makkah today

5

Makkah in ancient times

Desert mountains around Makkah

Makkah has been an important **holy** place for thousands of years. Muslims believe that the **prophet** Aadam built the first house of **Allah** there, thousands of years before Muhammad (**pbuh**) was born.

Many years later, the prophet Ibrahim lived in the area with his wife, Hajra. The **Qur'an** tells how Hajra was stranded alone in the hot desert with her baby son, Isma'il. Soon the baby needed water. Hajra ran between the hills, searching for water. Suddenly, Hajra saw water bubbling out of the ground. A **miracle** had saved her baby. The spring became known as the Well of Zamzam. Later, Ibrahim built a holy building there. That building was called the Ka'bah.

Street stalls selling food to **pilgrims** on **Hajj**, as in ancient times

Makkah grew up around the Well and the Ka'bah. Desert tribes-people visited the Ka'bah as a holy place. Great fairs were held nearby each year, and traders sold costly spices and jewels.

The Bible and the Qur'an

Muslims believe that Muhammad (pbuh) was the last in a long line of prophets sent to Earth by Allah. Many of the same prophets appear in the **Jewish** holy book called the **Hebrew Bible**. This is holy to **Christians**, too, who call it the Old Testament.

Names in Bible	Names in Qur'an
Adam	Aadam
Abraham	Ibrahim
Hagar	Hajra
Ishmael	Isma'il
Gabriel	Jibril

Who was the prophet Muhammad (pbuh)?

In about 570 CE, the **prophet** Muhammad (**pbuh**) was born in Makkah. Muhammad (pbuh) was born into a wealthy family. He grew up to be kind and honest. People called him Al-Amin, which means 'the trustworthy one'.

Muhammad (pbuh) hated to see people worshipping many different gods, and fighting and cheating the poor. He started to go out into the desert beyond Makkah to think and **pray**.

One night, in the desert, Muhammad (pbuh) was visited by the Angel Jibril. Jibril carried a piece of cloth with writing on it. Muhammad (pbuh) found that he could read the words, although he had never learned to read or write.

Pilgrims visiting the cave where Muhammad (pbuh) stayed in the desert

People from the desert travelling with camels like they did in the time of Muhammad (pbuh)

These words were the first part of the Muslim **holy** book, the **Qur'an**. The angel returned several times to tell Muhammad (pbuh) the rest of the Qur'an.

After that, Muhammad (pbuh) spent his time teaching people about **Allah**. But many people in Makkah did not want to listen. In 622 CE Muhammad (pbuh) travelled from Makkah to live and teach in another city called Madinah. His followers there became the first Muslims.

The hijrah and the Muslim calendar

The hijrah is the name for the journey Muhammad (pbuh) made from Makkah to Madinah in 622 CE. It was so important that the Muslim calendar starts from this year. Muslim years are followed by AH, which comes from words that mean 'year of the hijrah'.

9

What is Makkah's history?

From the age of 40 Muhammad (**pbuh**) spent his life teaching about **Allah** and **Islam**. He died in 632 CE. After his death, Islam spread quickly to the lands around the Mediterranean Sea. Makkah became the most important place for Muslims everywhere.

Pilgrims came there on **pilgrimage**, or **Hajj**, from all over the world. The pilgrims spent money and so Makkah grew rich, as local people sold goods to the people on Hajj.

The Great **Mosque** in Makkah, surrounded by modern buildings

DID YOU KNOW?

Muhammad (pbuh) spoke Arabic, the language of Saudi Arabia. The **Qur'an** is written in Arabic. Arabic letters are different from the letters used to write English. In this book, English letters are used to spell Arabic words. Sometimes different spellings are used for the same sound. For example, Makkah can be written Mecca. The spellings used in this book give the sound that is closest to the sound of the Arabic word.

There have been many battles for control of the land around Makkah. In the centuries after the death of Muhammad (pbuh), Arab rulers, called the Abbasids were in control. Later, Turkish rulers called the Ottomans took over. They were in control for hundreds of years.

In 1932, the kingdom in which Makkah lies was renamed Saudi Arabia. Saudi Arabia is a rich country, because it produces and sells oil.

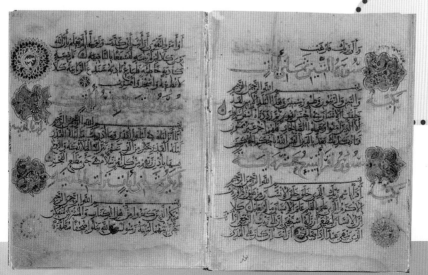

Arabic writing in the Qur'an

What is the Great Mosque at Makkah?

The Great **Mosque** is the most important **religious** building in Makkah. Around 500,000 people can fit inside it. The Great Mosque has towers called minarets at each corner. From the minarets, the **muezzin**, or caller, calls people to **prayer**.

The Mosque is surrounded by a great wall. The area inside the wall is called the Haram or **holy** enclosure. Inside the Haram is a huge open courtyard, paved with white marble. At its centre is the Ka'bah, an ancient building in the shape of a huge cube.

Pilgrims praying around the Ka'bah

The Ka'bah covered with its decorated cloth. The towers behind it are minarets.

The Ka'bah is 15 metres (49 feet) high. It is built of stone, and on one side has a brass door decorated with religious writings from the **Qur'an**. There is a holy black stone in one corner of the Ka'bah. The Ka'bah is covered with a beautiful cloth embroidered with religious writings. Next to the Ka'bah is Hajra's grave, and the graves of other **prophets**.

The Great Mosque is a modern building. It has been rebuilt many times over the centuries, each time to make a new and beautiful building to worship **Allah**. Rebuilding has made it safer for the millions of **pilgrims** who come to Makkah on **Hajj**.

What is Hajj ?

Hajj is the journey to Makkah, and is one of the most important things that Muslims believe in. It is one of the 'Five Pillars of **Islam**', which are explained later on page 22.

Before they set off, Muslims get ready for going on Hajj. They say special **prayers** and study the rules for living on Hajj.

Pilgrims travel to Makkah from countries all over the world. Some people save up money over many years to make the journey. In the past, many pilgrims from faraway countries travelled over land and sea for months or even years to reach Makkah.

Pilgrims and their luggage at Jeddah airport on the journey to Makkah

These pilgrims are making their way to Makkah on foot

Today most pilgrims travel to Saudi Arabia by aeroplane. They arrive at Jeddah airport. Then it is a coach journey of about 75 kilometres (47 miles) to Makkah. City officials make special travel arrangements so that all the people can arrive safely on Hajj. Special bus stops and information centres are set up. Police patrol to help travellers and to make sure there is no trouble. There is even a special postal system set up for the period of Hajj.

A long journey

Air travel has made going on Hajj easier than before. Even so, it can still be a long and tiring journey to reach Makkah. But pilgrims see this journey as a **symbol** of their journey towards **Allah**. They do not expect it to be an easy journey.

On Hajj at Makkah

Over 2 million people arrive at Makkah on **Hajj** each year. They come during the Muslim month of Dhul-Hijja. All the **pilgrims** wear simple white robes called ihram. Dressing simply shows that everyone, rich or poor, is equal before **Allah**.

A whole city of tents is set up for people to stay in. While they are on Hajj, pilgrims must live very simply. They should not kill any animals or insects or plants, and they must not do anything unkind or dishonest to anyone. Husbands and wives must stay apart during Hajj.

A city of tents set up for pilgrims to stay in

First, pilgrims enter the Great **Mosque** for **prayers**. They walk barefoot around the Ka'bah seven times, saying special prayers to Allah as they go.

Next the pilgrims drink water from the Well of Zamzam. After that they walk or run seven times along the valley between the hills of Al-Safa and Al-Marwa. As they do this, they remember how Hajra ran there searching for water to save her baby son.

The valley between the hills used to be a dusty, open area crowded with shops and traffic. Now it is a paved and covered corridor, so that pilgrims are sheltered as they walk up and down.

This plan shows the way pilgrims follow when on Hajj

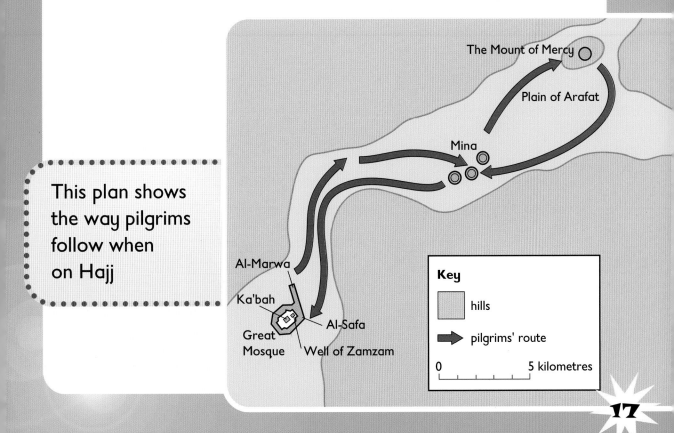

The Mount of Mercy

Plain of Arafat

Mina

Al-Marwa

Ka'bah

Al-Safa

Great Mosque

Well of Zamzam

Key

hills

pilgrims' route

0   5 kilometres

On Hajj beyond Makkah

Next the **pilgrims** travel about 25 kilometres (16 miles) outside Makkah to Mount Arafat, the Mount of Mercy. There, they ask **Allah** to forgive their **sins**. This is called wuquf, or 'standing before Allah'. It is the most important part of **Hajj**. Pilgrims hope that Allah will forgive all the bad things they have done throughout their life.

The last stop of the Hajj is at Mina. This is where Satan, the devil, appeared to the **prophet** Ibrahim as he was trying to **pray**. Ibrahim threw seven pebbles at the devil who sank down defeated to the ground. The devil appeared twice more, and each time Ibrahim threw seven pebbles at him and defeated him. The three stone pillars at Mina are **symbols** of the devil. Pilgrims gather small pebbles to throw at the pillars, to show that they reject the devil and his evil ways, as Ibrahim did long ago.

Pilgrims on Mount Arafat

One of the stone pillars at Mina. Some of the pilgrims are throwing pebbles.

Id-ul-Adha is one of the main Muslim festivals. It falls during the Hajj. At this festival, Muslims remember how Ibrahim sacrificed a ram. You can read the story below. At Id-ul-Adha, pilgrims pay to give food to the poor.

At the end of the Hajj, pilgrims can relax a little after the simple life on Hajj.

Ibrahim and Isma'il

The **Qur'an** tells how Allah told Ibrahim to **sacrifice** his beloved son, Isma'il. Because he loved Allah, Ibrahim wanted to obey. Just in time, Ibraham heard the voice of Allah telling him to stop, and to sacrifice a ram instead of his son. Ibrahim had proved his love of Allah, and Isma'il was safe.

19

When I went on Hajj

Hasina, a Muslim woman from Birmingham, remembers going on **Hajj** to Makkah as a young woman.

*I saved all my money for the first year that I worked, until I could afford to go on Hajj. I travelled to Makkah with my brother and some other people from our **mosque**. I was a bit worried, but excited too!*

At first, I was surprised that the Ka'bah was inside such a modern building. I expected to see more of the desert. But then, as I got used to it, tears came to my eyes and all my worries seemed to fall away.

African women **pilgrims** arriving at Makkah

I felt very happy on Hajj. All the **prayers** and rituals help you to find peace inside yourself. God gives you strength to bear the great heat and crowds. The hardship makes you feel stronger. I worried less about ordinary things, such as what other people might be thinking. Everybody looks after one another.

We bought bottles of Zamzam water to take home as gifts. Being at home felt strange for a while, after such a simple life of prayer. Just talking about Hajj makes me long to be at Makkah again!

More about Islam

The Five Pillars of **Islam** are the five most important ways Muslims keep their **religion**. They are not real, solid pillars, but are the five basic **beliefs** of Islam. All Muslims should follow each of the five beliefs. You can read the Five Pillars of Islam below.

Muslims often go to the **mosque** to **pray**, although they can pray anywhere as long as it is clean. 'All the world is a mosque,' said the **prophet** Muhammad (**pbuh**).

At the mosque, men pray together in a large, open room. Women may pray in a different part of the room or in another room, or at home.

The Five Pillars of Islam

- **Faith**: Muslims believe that there is no God but **Allah**, and Muhammad (pbuh) is his prophet
- Prayer: Muslims pray five times each day, facing Makkah
- Charity: giving money to the poor
- Fasting: going without food or drink during daylight, throughout the month of Ramadan
- **Pilgrimage**: or going on **Hajj** to Makkah. Muslims must do this once during their lifetime.

Muslim prayers follow a set pattern, with movements including bowing, kneeling and bending down to touch the floor with your forehead. Different prayers are said in each position. Everyone moves and says the same prayers together. In their prayers, Muslims worship **Allah** and ask **blessings** for Muhammad (pbuh) and for all Muslims.

The most important Muslim prayer is called the shahada. Translated into English, it means:
There is no God but Allah and
Muhammad is the Messenger of Allah.

Children learning in a class at a mosque

Through the Muslim year

The month of Ramadan is special to Muslims. Every year during Ramadan Muslims fast. This means they do not eat or drink anything during the hours of sunlight. Muslims believe that it is good to have control over your body. Making yourself wait to eat, even when you are hungry, is one way of showing this control. Fasting is a reminder that everyone is equal. Hunger is the same for everyone, whether they are rich or poor.

A family breaking their fast during Ramadan

Muslim months and years

The Muslim calendar is based on the Moon, instead of the Sun and the seasons, like the Western calendar. The Muslim year is about eleven days shorter because each month is shorter. So each year, Muslim festivals fall on an earlier date according to the Western calendar.

At the end of the month of Ramadan is the festival of Id-ul-Fitr. This is a great celebration, when families gather together for a special meal to end the fast. People go to visit friends and relatives at Id-ul-Fitr. They may have new clothes to wear, and bring small presents of sweets or nuts for the children.

The Muslim New Year comes on the Day of the Hijrah. This is the first day of the Muslim month of Muharram. On this day, Muslims remember the journey made by Muhammad (**pbuh**) to Madinah.

The Moon rising over the **mosque** at Dubai, United Arab Emirates

25

Other Muslim holy places: Madinah

Madinah is the second most important place for Muslims. It is known as the 'city of light'. Madinah is also in Saudi Arabia. It is about 320 kilometres (about 199 miles) north of Makkah. It gets more rain than the harsh desert around Makkah. Madinah is green with many trees.

The story goes that when the **prophet** Muhammad (**pbuh**) arrived at Madinah many people offered him shelter and land. But Muhammad (pbuh) did not want to be a burden to anyone, and he did not want to seem to choose someone over everybody else. Instead, he said that he would build his own house, on the spot where his camel decided to stop.

Madinah is cooler and greener than Makkah

This mosque is built at the grave of Muhammad (pbuh)

Everyone followed the camel to see where it would stop. Then Muhammad (pbuh) bought that piece of land, and his followers helped him to build a house there.

When Muhammad (pbuh) died in 632 CE, he was buried at Madinah. A beautiful **mosque** is built at the site of his grave. **Pilgrims** come to visit and **pray** there.

The first Hajj

Muhammad (pbuh) went to Madinah because the people of Makkah were angry. They did not want to follow his teaching. Then, six years later, he returned to Makkah and marched with his followers straight to the Ka'bah. At last the people of Makkah accepted his teachings. This journey back to Makkah became the first pilgrimage or **Hajj**.

27

Other Muslim holy places: Jerusalem

The Dome of the Rock, a mosque in Jerusalem

Jerusalem, in the modern country of Israel, is the third most **holy** place for Muslims. A **mosque** with a golden dome, called the Dome of the Rock, is built where the **prophet** Muhammad (**pbuh**) was lifted up to heaven when he made his Night Journey.

Muhammad's Night Journey

It is said that one night in Makkah, the Angel Jibril visited the prophet Muhammad (pbuh). This time, Jibril brought a strange beast, called Buraq, for Muhammad (pbuh) to ride. Buraq had wings and could gallop faster than lightning. Muhammad (pbuh) mounted Buraq and in a single second he was taken to Jerusalem. He sat on Mount Moriah, where Ibrahim had bound Isma'il for **sacrifice**. Slowly, Muhammad (pbuh) rose to heaven. There he talked to Aadam, Ibrahim and Isa (Jesus). That is why Jerusalem is **sacred** for Muslims.

The Al-Aqsa mosque nearby has a silver dome. The two domes can be seen from all around Jerusalem. This is the spot where Muhammad (pbuh) is said to have landed after his Night Journey on Buraq.

Jerusalem is a holy city for **Jews** and **Christians** as well. Through the centuries, there have been times when people of different **religions** have lived and worshipped side by side peacefully there. But there has often been conflict, too. Even today, people are still fighting there.

The Al-Aqsa Mosque stands in Jerusalem, facing the Dome of the Rock

Glossary

Allah   Muslim name for God

beliefs   when you think or know something to be true

CE   stands for the Common Era. People of all religions can use this, instead of the Christian AD that counts from the birth of Jesus Christ. The year numbers are not changed.

Christian   someone who follows the religion of Christianity and the teachings of Jesus Christ

faith   belief in God or Allah

Hajj   Muslim name for the holy journey or pilgrimage to Makkah

Hebrew Bible   Jewish holy book

holy (holiest)   to do with God

Islam   religion of Muslims

Jews (Jewish)   someone who follows the religion of Judaism

Middle East   lands around the east and south of the Mediterranean Sea, including countries such as Saudi Arabia, Israel, Egypt, Iran and Iraq

miracle   something that God made happen

mosque   Muslim place of worship, sometimes also called a masjid

muezzin   Muslim man who calls people to prayer

pbuh   letters stand for 'peace be upon him'

pilgrimage   journey made for religious reasons

pilgrim   someone making a pilgrimage

pray/prayer   to think about or talk to God or Allah. A prayer is the words you think or say when you pray.

prophet   someone who tells people what God or Allah wants

Qur'an   Muslim holy book

religion (**religious**)   belief in God or gods

sacrifice   offering something to God or Allah

sin   doing something wrong, against the teachings of God or Allah

symbol   sign, or something that stands for something else

Index

Titles in the *Holy Places* series:

Hardback   0 431 15510 0

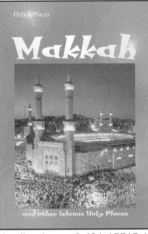

Hardback   0 431 15515 1

Hardback   0 431 15511 9

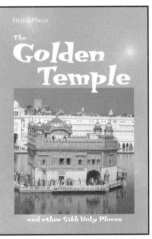

Hardback   0 431 15512 7

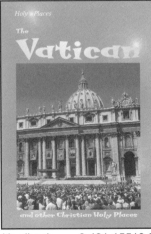

Hardback   0 431 15513 5

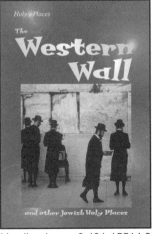

Hardback   0 431 15514 3

Find out about other Heinemann titles on our website www.heinemann.co.uk/library